How to Draw
Amazing
Animals
and Incredible Insects

BARRON'S

Created and produced by Green Android Ltd

Illustrated by Fiona Gowen

First edition for North America
published in 2015 by
Barron's Educational Series, Inc.

Copyright © Green Android Ltd 2012

Green Android Ltd
49 Beaumont Court
Upper Clapton Road
London E5 8BG
United Kingdom
www.greenandroid.co.uk

All inquiries should be addressed to:
Barron's Educational Series, Inc.
250 Wireless Boulevard
Hauppauge, NY 11788
www.barronseduc.com

ISBN: 978-1-4380-0583-6

Date of Manufacture: July 2015
Manufactured by:
Toppan Leefung Printing Co., Ltd.,
Dongguan, China

Printed in China
9 8 7 6 5 4 3 2

Contents

 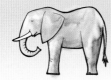
See page 32 for an index of all the animals in this book.

Colorful Fish

There are thousands of types of fish in our rivers and oceans. You can use different styles and colors to make a fun underwater scene.

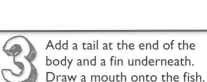

1 Start with the eye of the fish. Draw a circle with a dot in it.

2 Draw a long thin body and a curved face. Leave a gap in the lines for the tail, fins, and mouth.

3 Add a tail at the end of the body and a fin underneath. Draw a mouth onto the fish.

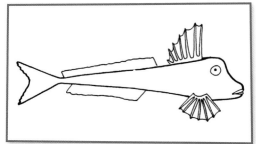

4 Draw two thin fins running along the body and large fins above and below the face.

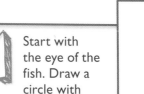

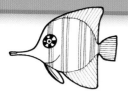

More to Draw
Fish come in different shapes, sizes, and patterns.
Try drawing some of these amazing fish.

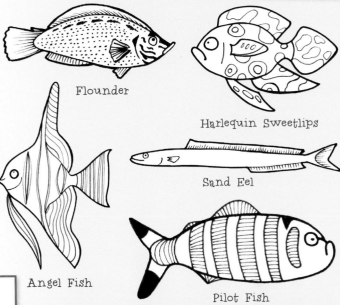

Flounder

Harlequin Sweetlips

Sand Eel

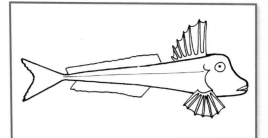

 Draw a curved line around the face and a long thin line down the entire length of the body.

Angel Fish

Pilot Fish

Dogfish

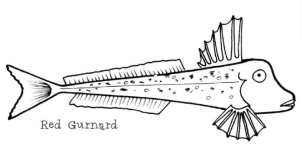

Red Gurnard

 Add the final details to the fish. Include small lines on the fins and tail. Add lots of dots to the body.

Sea Dragon

Sunfish

Parrot Fish

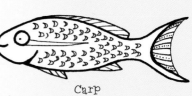

Carp

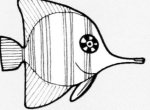

Butterfly Fish

Littlehead Porgy

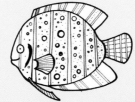
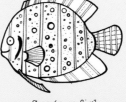

Surgeonfish

How to Draw
Fluttering Beauties

Butterflies and moths have large, often brightly colored wings. They eat the nectar from flowers and are ideal for adding to drawings of gardens.

1 Start your drawing with a small circle and an oval.

2 Add a section of segments below the oval shape. This will become the body of your butterfly.

3 Draw some large wings coming out of either side of the butterfly's body.

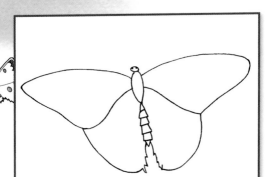

4 Add some antennae to the head and begin decorating the butterfly's wings.

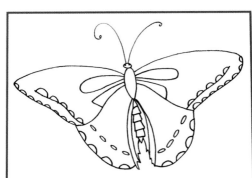

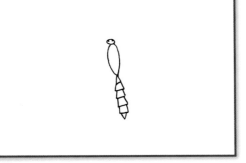

6

Butterflies and moths have beautiful patterned wings. Try drawing some of these pretty examples.

Blue Morpho

Mountain Ringlet

5 Continue to add more details to the wings. Make sure you give the wings symmetrical patterns.

Purple-edged Copper

Peacock

Monarch

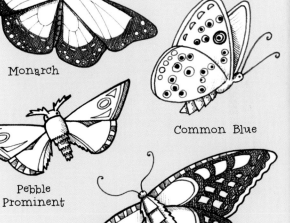

Common Blue

Painted Lady

Pebble Prominent

6 To finish your butterfly drawing, add some shading to the patterns on each of the wings.

Swallowtail

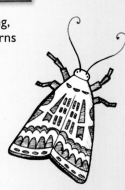

Ashworth's Rustic

Cream-bordered Green Pea

Water Ermine

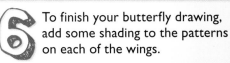

How to Draw

Woodland Wonders

Owls live in trees and only come out during the night. These birds make great additions to drawings of forests and woodlands.

1 Start with a heart-shaped face, two big eyes, and a small beak.

2 Draw a big oval shape around the owl's face. Make the bottom of the oval curve inward for the owl's feet.

3 Add some feet, wings, and ears to the owl's feathery body.

Mouse

Hedgehog

4 Add some feathery details around the beak and then begin decorating the owl's face and body.

Great Horned Owl

6 To finish your owl, shade the top of its head and areas around its face, ears, and body.

5 Shade some of the patterned areas on your owl's body. Also shade some patterns around the face.

Snail

Mole

Tropical Fliers

There are hundreds of tropical birds, including parrots, hornbills, toucans, and eagles. These colorful birds are great for forest and jungle drawings.

1 Draw two small eyes and a triangular shaped beak.

2 Add a feathery face and body. Draw two claws onto the body.

3 Draw a branch for the bird to sit on and some long feathers for its tail.

4 Now add plumes around the face. Draw some outlines for the wings.

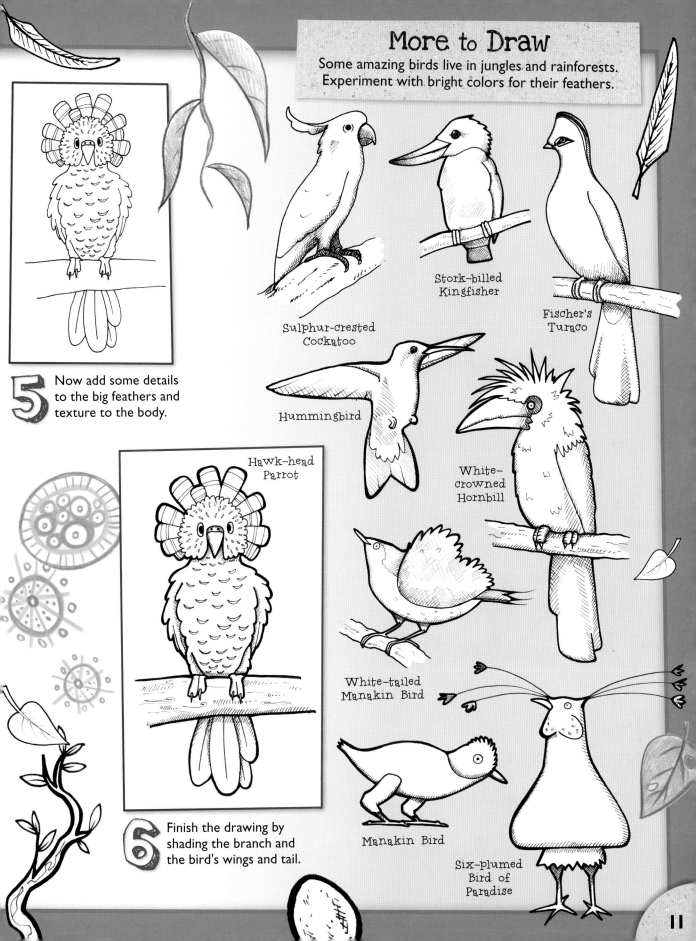

More to Draw

Some amazing birds live in jungles and rainforests.
Experiment with bright colors for their feathers.

Sulphur-crested
Cockatoo

Stork-billed
Kingfisher

Fischer's
Turaco

Hummingbird

White-
crowned
Hornbill

White-tailed
Manakin Bird

Manakin Bird

Six-plumed
Bird of
Paradise

5 Now add some details
to the big feathers and
texture to the body.

Hawk-head
Parrot

6 Finish the drawing by
shading the branch and
the bird's wings and tail.

Graceful Giraffes

Giraffes are the tallest land animals in the world.
They live in Africa's savannas, grasslands, and
woodlands. Draw them near trees
because they eat leaves.

1 Draw a box shape for the face and a long line for the neck. Add an eye to the face.

2 Now draw the ears on either side of the giraffe's face.

3 Draw a square shape for the snout and two little horns. Draw a line to form the neck and back.

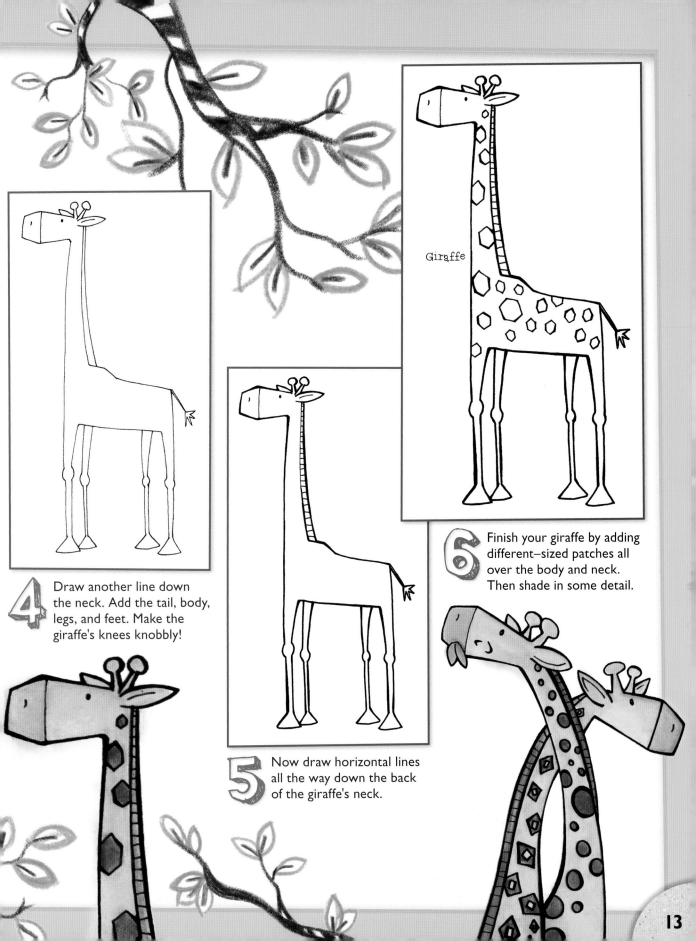

Giraffe

4 Draw another line down the neck. Add the tail, body, legs, and feet. Make the giraffe's knees knobbly!

5 Now draw horizontal lines all the way down the back of the giraffe's neck.

6 Finish your giraffe by adding different-sized patches all over the body and neck. Then shade in some detail.

How to Draw
Terrific Tigers

Tigers are the largest of all of the big cats. They are found in South and Southeast Asia and are known for their beautiful striped fur.

1 Draw a long rectangular face. Add some ears and a triangular nose.

2 Add the body and legs. Remember to add a curved tail. Shade inside the tiger's ears.

3 Now draw stripes over the body and legs. Add some triangle shapes to the face.

4 Shade the triangles on the tiger's face and some of the stripes on the body and legs.

5 Draw small triangles, dots, and blocks between some of the stripes on the tiger's body and legs.

Tiger

6 To finish the drawing, you can add even more patterns. Try adding tiny dots along some of the stripes.

15

How to Draw
Incredible Leapers

Frogs and toads are great jumpers and swimmers. These little creatures can add lovely detail to your drawings of ponds, rivers, and jungle scenes.

1 Start with a big circle for an eye and then draw a line around half of it.

2 Add a curved line for the frog's back. Draw lines for the other eye, mouth, and chin.

3 Now add some thin back legs. Draw a small circle at the end of each toe.

4 Draw the front legs bending forward and add a line for the belly.

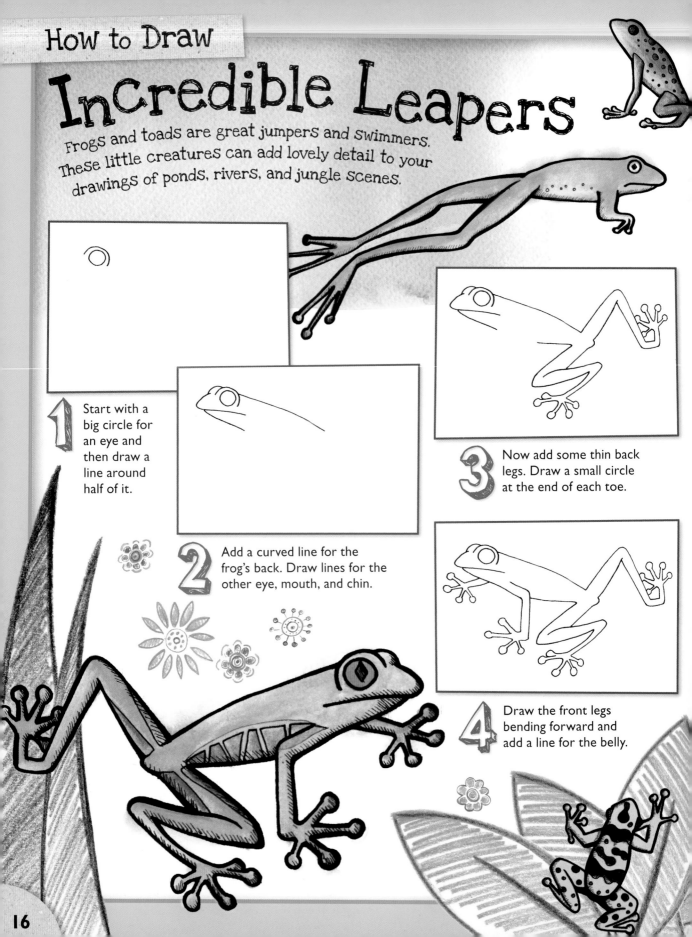

More to Draw

There are many different types of frogs and toads.
Try drawing some of the examples below.

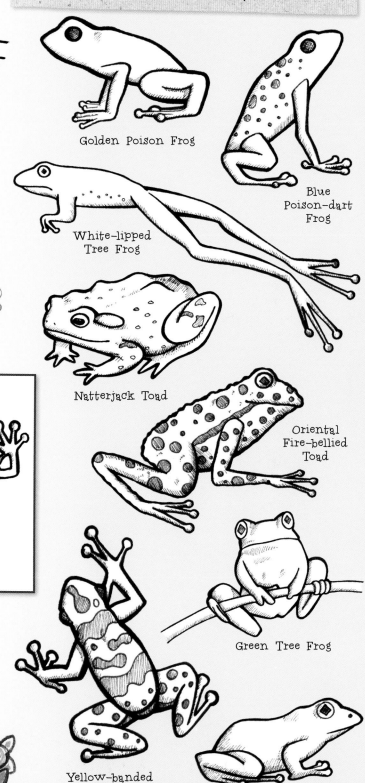

Golden Poison Frog

Blue
Poison-dart
Frog

White-lipped
Tree Frog

Natterjack Toad

Oriental
Fire-bellied
Toad

5 Decorate your frog with shapes along the belly and then add a diamond shape in the eye.

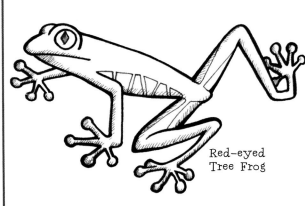

Red-eyed
Tree Frog

6 Use a pencil to shade some areas of the frog—this will help to make your frog drawing look more realistic.

Green Tree Frog

Yellow-banded
Poison-dart Frog

Brown Tree Frog

How to Draw

African Giants

These huge animals live in grasslands, forests, deserts, and mountains. They live in large family herds, so why not make a drawing of a group of elephants?

African Fish Eagle

1 Start your drawing with a triangular ear, an eye, and a curved line for the back and top of the head.

2 Add two large legs and a small curved line to make the chin.

3 Draw the large tusk and the curved trunk.

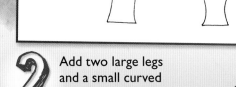

Impala

Zebra

4 Now add the belly and tail to the elephant.

Elephant

5 Use a pencil to make the outline thicker. Add lines around the trunk and knees.

6 Finally, shade around the belly, legs, ear, and trunk to create a realistic look.

How to Draw
Sticky InSects

These strange-looking insects use camouflage to hide from predators. They are great to hide in pictures containing leaves and foliage.

1 Draw a curved shape for wings and a line for the body.

2 Add two thin walking legs and grasping legs in front of the insect's body.

3 Now draw two large eyes and an outline for the insect's face.

4 Draw antennae coming out of the insect's head and add a back set of walking legs. Now draw the front grasping legs.

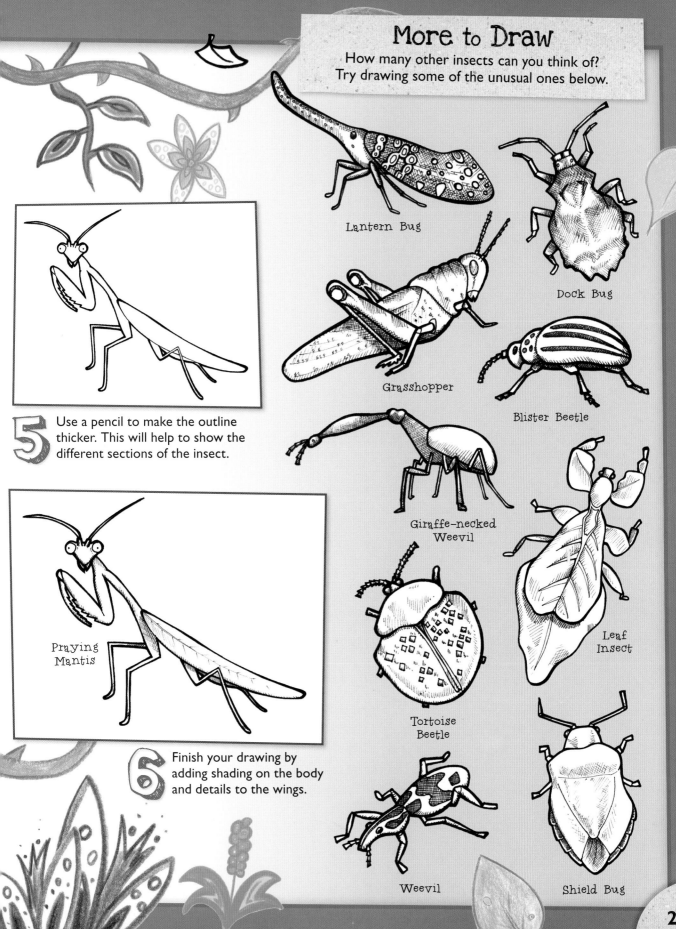

More to Draw

How many other insects can you think of?
Try drawing some of the unusual ones below.

Lantern Bug

Dock Bug

Grasshopper

Blister Beetle

5 Use a pencil to make the outline thicker. This will help to show the different sections of the insect.

Giraffe-necked Weevil

Praying Mantis

Leaf Insect

Tortoise Beetle

6 Finish your drawing by adding shading on the body and details to the wings.

Weevil

Shield Bug

How to Draw

Fluffy Friends

It is always fun to draw pictures of your pets and the animals that belong to your friends and family. You can give your drawings to the owners as gifts.

1 Draw a triangle nose and fluffy outline for the dog's head.

2 Continue the fluffy outline up over the dog's nose. Draw the dog's eye underneath the fur.

3 Draw fluffy fur on either side of the nose. Add more fur around the dog's face.

4 Now you can draw the outline of the dog's body. Draw it as a wavy line to show it is furry.

More to Draw

People keep many different types of animals as pets.
Practice copying some of the pets below.

5 Add some furry lines across the body of the dog. This will make different sections to shade in.

Old English Sheepdog

6 To finish the drawing, shade some areas darker and add some texture to the fur on the dog's body.

Ferret

Hamster

Rabbit

Pug

Gerbil

Cat

Guinea Pig

Chinchilla

Llama

How to Draw
Icy Animals

There are different types of penguins that live all over the world, but the most famous are the Emperor penguins that live in the Antarctic.

Gull

1 Draw a large oval outline. Add the head and feet.

2 Now add wings to either side of the body and two webbed feet.

3 Draw a curved shape around the penguin's face and add a small eye.

Polar Bear

Narwhal

Minke Whale

4 Add details to the beak and along the penguin's shoulders and wings.

Emperor Penguin

6 Finish by adding shadows along the outline of the body and under the wings.

5 Now you can shade in the face, beak, and wings. Don't forget to shade in the penguin's feet.

Arctic Hare

Walrus

How to Draw
Exotic Lizards

There are thousands of lizards, from tiny geckos to huge Komodo Dragons. Some lizards can change their color to blend in with their surroundings.

1 Draw lines for the face and chin, and a curved back.

2 Now add the front leg. Make sure the toes are long and pointy.

3 Draw a back leg with the same pointy toes as you drew on the front leg.

4 Draw a curved tail and belly. Add a flap of skin under the chin. This is called a dewlap.

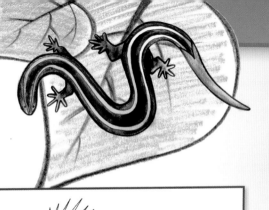

More to Draw
Lizards can be found in places all over the world.
Practice drawing some of these different lizards.

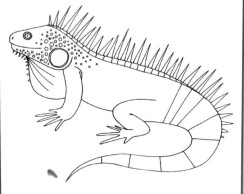

5 Now draw the spiky crest along the iguana's back. Add dots to the face and neck and stripes to the tail.

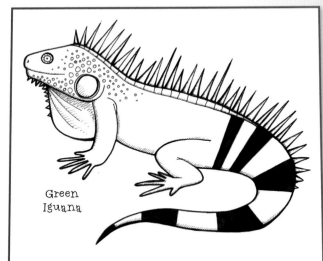

Green Iguana

6 Finish your iguana by shading stripes down the tail and adding shadows to the underside of the body and neck.

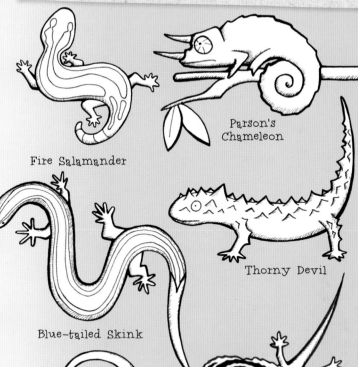

Fire Salamander

Parson's Chameleon

Blue-tailed Skink

Thorny Devil

Madagascar Day Gecko

Flying Dragon

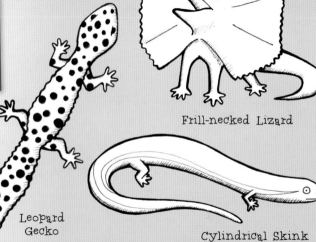

Leopard Gecko

Frill-necked Lizard

Cylindrical Skink

How to Draw
Amazing Swimmers

There are some very fierce-looking animals swimming around our seas, rivers, and oceans. Sharks are probably the most feared of all the animals in the ocean.

1 Start the drawing with a long oval shape with a tail at the end.

2 Draw a small black eye and then add some fins along the top and bottom of the body.

3 Now go over the outline again with your pencil to make it really stand out.

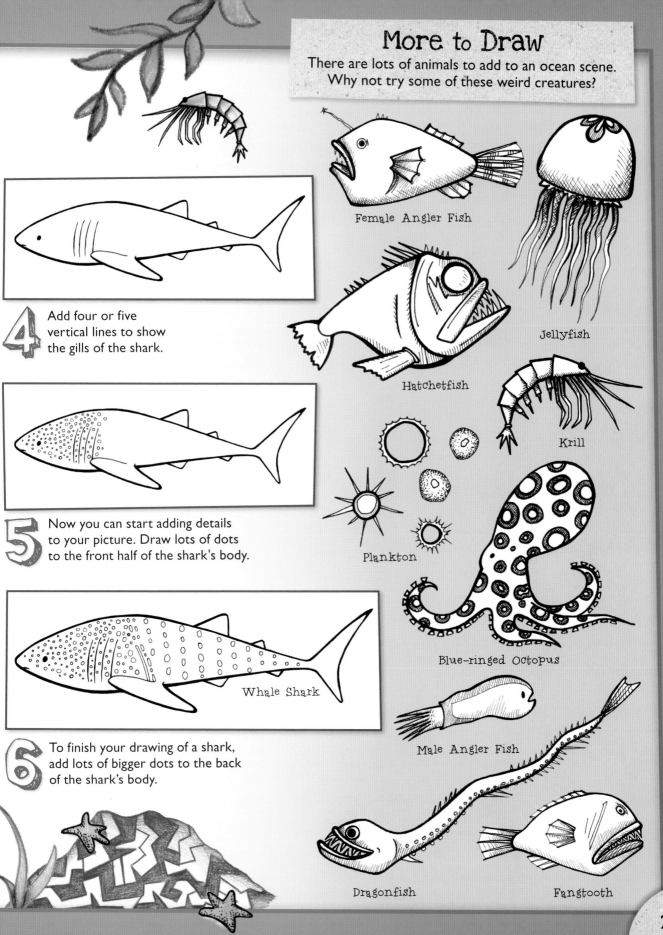

More to Draw

There are lots of animals to add to an ocean scene.
Why not try some of these weird creatures?

Female Angler Fish

Jellyfish

Hatchetfish

Krill

Plankton

Blue-ringed Octopus

Male Angler Fish

Whale Shark

Dragonfish

Fangtooth

4 Add four or five vertical lines to show the gills of the shark.

5 Now you can start adding details to your picture. Draw lots of dots to the front half of the shark's body.

6 To finish your drawing of a shark, add lots of bigger dots to the back of the shark's body.

How to Draw
Slippery Snakes

Snakes are fun to draw because you can design wild patterns all over their skin. You can add them to drawings of deserts, jungles, and woodlands.

Tree Snake

1 Start with a basic outline for the snake. Make the tail into a point.

2 Now add extra lines inside the outline. This is to show the snake's belly.

3 Decorate the belly of the snake by adding stripes.

4 Make the outline thicker by drawing over the lines again. Add a thin, forked tongue.

Brown Tree Snake

Eastern Tiger Snake

Coral Snake

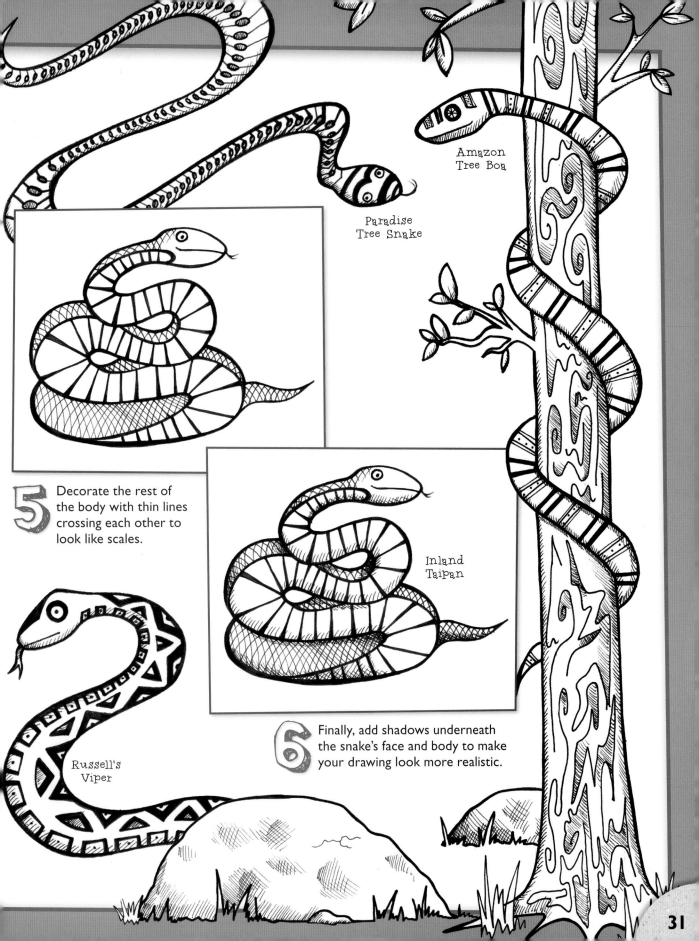

Amazon
Tree Boa

Paradise
Tree Snake

5 Decorate the rest of the body with thin lines crossing each other to look like scales.

Inland
Taipan

6 Finally, add shadows underneath the snake's face and body to make your drawing look more realistic.

Russell's
Viper

Animal Index

There are over one hundred different animals in this book. Practice your newfound drawing skills by adding some of them to your drawings.